# A POCKET FULL OF EMPOWERMENT: A COLLECTION OF THE BEST INSPIRING SHORT STORIES

## VAIKHARI CHAVAN NAIK

I DEDICATE THIS BOOK TO MY BROTHER WHO I LOST
IN 2023. NIKU, YOU ARE TRULY LOVED EVEN THOUGH
YOU FELT ALONE MOST TIMES, WE WERE ALWAYS
WITH YOU. I WISH I COULD BE THERE WHENEVER
YOU NEEDED ME. I WISH I COULD HOLD YOUR HAND
AND BRING YOU INTO SUNSHINE WHEN THINGS
WERE DARKEST FOR YOU. I MISS YOU EVERY DAY AND
I WILL ALWAYS LOVE YOU FOREVER. HOPE YOU ARE AT
PEACE WHEREVER YOU ARE.

MY DEAR AGASTYA,
YOU ARE THE SUNSHINE OF OUR LIVES, THE RAY OF
HOPE AND INNOCENCE GIFTED TO US. MOM AND DAD
LOVE YOU A LOT. IN DARKER TIMES, LET THIS BOOK
GUIDE YOU AND GIVE YOU SOME SUNSHINE

# Contents

# Contents

# FOREWORD

In a world that moves at lightning speed, we often forget to pause, reflect, and find meaning in the everyday moments that shape us. This book is a gentle reminder of the power of stories—real, honest, and deeply human.

Each story in this collection is a spark—drawn from personal experiences, reflections, and heartfelt observations. These aren't grand tales of conquest or revolution, but simple, powerful vignettes that remind us of who we are and who we can become. They whisper truths we often overlook: the courage found in quiet persistence, the beauty in resilience, and the growth born from everyday struggles.

As you turn these pages, you may find a piece of your own journey reflected here. You may rediscover hope, clarity, or even a long-lost sense of purpose. That is the magic of stories born from lived experience—they resonate beyond words.

It is with immense joy and humility that I invite you to step into these stories. Let them inspire you, comfort you, and above all, remind you that you are not alone in your journey.

— Vaikhari

# PREFACE

This book was born from a quiet place within—a space shaped by years of personal experiences, silent observations, and moments that taught me more than any classroom or lecture ever could. Over time, I began collecting these stories—not just as memories, but as reflections of lessons learned, emotions felt, and transformations lived.

Each chapter in this collection is inspired by real events, either from my own life or from those who crossed my path. These stories may be simple, but their impact has been lasting. They taught me about courage in vulnerability, strength in compassion, and the quiet power of perseverance.

I do not claim to have all the answers. This is not a manual, but a mirror—offering glimpses of life's many shades. My hope is that in reading these pages, you'll find stories that speak to your own heart. Maybe you'll laugh, maybe you'll cry, but most importantly, I hope you'll pause to reflect and carry something meaningful with you.

This book is my way of saying: You are not alone. We're all walking our own paths, but sometimes, a story is all it takes to light the way forward.

With Warmth,

Vaikhari

# Acknowledgements

No journey is ever truly walked alone, and this book is no exception. As I look back on the stories within these pages, I am filled with gratitude for the many hearts and hands that helped shape them.

To my mother—your unwavering strength, kindness, and quiet wisdom have been the foundation of so many of my values and reflections.

To my brother and sisters—thank you for the shared memories, the laughter, the challenges, and the love that have added depth to my life and to these stories.

To my husband—your belief in me, your encouragement, and your calm presence have been an anchor through every step of this journey.

To my son—you are my greatest inspiration. Your curiosity, joy, and innocence remind me every day of the beauty in small moments.

To all the friends and family members whose stories, experiences, and quiet strength have found a place in these pages—thank you for trusting me, for listening, and for being part of this tapestry of inspiration.

This book is as much yours as it is mine. Thank you for walking beside me.

With love and gratitude,
Vaikhari

# Prologue

We often search for inspiration in distant places—in the words of great thinkers, in the triumphs of extraordinary people, or in the glow of dreams yet to be achieved. But more often than not, inspiration lives much closer. It hides in the quiet courage of everyday moments, in the choices we make without applause, and in the resilience we build through life's simplest trials.

This book is a celebration of those moments.

Each story you'll read is a reflection—sometimes of my own journey, sometimes of others around me—capturing the beauty, struggle, and wisdom embedded in real-life experiences. These are not fictional tales designed to entertain, but sincere accounts that aim to stir something within you: hope, strength, perspective, and perhaps a sense of belonging.

You don't need grand gestures to change your life. Sometimes, all it takes is one story that stays with you.

So as you begin this book, I invite you to read slowly, reflect deeply, and carry forward whatever speaks to your heart.

Let's begin.

— Vaikhari

# I

# What is the big deal about innocent people

*You are not a tree succumbed to the flow of the river, you
are a pillar trying to save those who need your support against
the challenging river*

Well, this is not a love focused or life message focused or career focused read. I'd say this read is from my heart and dedicated to all those people who have maintained to remain innocent, hopeful, dreamy, positive and strong even in the face of adversity. The world needs more people like this. Have you ever been through some situations which have changed you as a person? I was recently talking to my friend who was telling me about her breakup. More like reminiscing about that bad phase of her life. Maybe I am not the best relationship counsellor so I don't know if I could ease her pain. But I was able to feel that she was in pain even today. She was not crying. She was calmly telling me about how it affected her, how difficult it was and how it changed her as a person. She said that now she doesn't believe in 'all this love shit'. In her words, love is all false and 'impractical'.

And I was like, is this the same girl who used to think fairy tales about love stories, who had so many dreams and expectations for her love and life. I am a good listener but am not a very attentive one. However, I think more than just listening, it's the experience and learning that we should take from these little conversations in life. What is the hidden deep meaning behind the words that people say or behind their experiences, small or large, good or bad and how it helps us grow. In this particular conversation, I realised how some situations change people- not always for the better. But I also realised that ultimately it's the choice that we make on whether to 'allow' a situation to change us and in what manner? Upon going further deep on this thought, I understood the true meaning of strength. So when you think about strength of the mind, what do you think? Someone who looks tough, is a bit rude, says powerful words and doesn't show emotions, is strong? Well, my perspective about this has changed. Have you ever seen a tree standing strong in the middle of the river? Many trees who are in the middle of the river almost bend to the flow of the river. Because the force of the water makes it curved. This tree that looks strong from the outside standing alone in the river, is actually weak because slowly, it is being extracted from its roots. I think that if we consider the river as an adverse situation and that tree as a person, don't you think this person is weak? Almost every time we hear people talking about how situations change them, makes them tougher, makes them 'solid', makes them less vulnerable and create a tough outside shell, I feel that it's not that they have become strong. Infact, they have become a little less themselves.

The earlier vulnerable, simpler, happier version of them has now become a more complex, guarded, strategic version that thinks so much before doing every small thing. Is that really strong? Nope, it's weak because it's a mask. A mask that we tend to hide ourselves in thinking that we need to show this tough shell to people so that they don't hurt us. If I act tough, people will not mess with me. Well, hold that thought there. Now imagine a person, who has been through many heart breaks, seen many adversities but still believes that love exists, that life is not bad, it's just some days that have been bad and there are better days ahead, that life doesn't change her/him but that it's him/her that changes life. I think that is someone powerful. Who remains themselves even in adversity. Who doesn't stop believing in the good because of some bad situations. People who remain good even after being surrounded by bad and people who don't let the darkness outside consume their light are truly strong. It's rare to meet people who shine bright even in a dark night, who remain innocent even when being faced constantly with corruption and who are determined to be happy even in the face of sadness. So what is the big deal about them? Well, they are not a ray of light or a candle in darkness. They are like the damn sun that is so bright and that you don't need to carry anywhere, but their brightness will illuminate your world wherever you go.

I'd say its easy to find a tree that changes its direction as per the flow of the river... but the one who remains their same undeterred, innocent, simple happy self after so many difficult situations are truly the ones who will brighten our world and these type of people are actually the big deal in our world ❤?❤?

# II

# Not just a star but a full galaxy...

*I've been destroyed a thousand ways, so now I know a thousand ways to rebuild myself!*

Recently I saw the movie 'Damsel' and oh my god I would definitely recommend it. Besides the fact that it was my favourite actress' movie and looking at all the amazing trailers (which already makes it a must watch), the story is refreshingly simple but powerful. Why simple, because the theme is about a girl who is betrayed by her partner and then she decides to be her own hero, a phenomenon which happens in our every day life and our every day films. But then what makes it powerful? Well according to me, the story is powerful because when at first her struggle is survival, by the end of the movie, she is a protector and a provider. In most stories like these either the main protagonists escape death or being eaten by the dragon OR they slay the dragon and become the name in their tribe. This story does much better. It is where the protagonist befriends the dragon, relates with the dragon's pain, goes beyond her walls of self pity and misery and actually looks at the magnificent creature though empathetic eyes.

Now I know, many of us will say that its stupid to befriend the beast who is ought to kill you, but going beyond logic I think it's important that we acknowledge her brave decision to bring justice to both her and the beast. Well and then ofcourse her decision to take on one heck of a fight and get outta that situation. There are many things that such movies teach us apart from just giving us that small dose of inspiration. Most times when someone wrongs us, our first instinct is to go into self-pity, put up our defences for everyone and try to get our revenge back on the person. When fate does not allow us to take revenge, we wallow more into self-pity. I think this is where we need to change our approach. Why waste our time and lower our vibe on things which are not going to matter in a few years. The self-pity, the revenge, the people who hurt us will fade away, so the time and energy we are putting into these momentary phases are not going to matter and not going to contribute towards building us.

However, there is one way in which we can use these phases to build us. Instead of throwing our energy into looking at the dark side of these phases, we need to work with the dark sides. We need to mould the dark sides and create one hell of a weapon to fight our demons. The demons that are inside us, that tell us that we are weak, that we need to pity our situation and realize how luck has been unfair, how things have been difficult and how we are always the victim to such situations. What's done is done but now that darkness is staring at us so we don't stare at it waiting for our turn to come to light, we take a handful of that darkness and start working with it to maybe build something inside us that'll get us out of the darkness. The first step towards our progression is not accepting anything less than we deserve. Now it's important to get to work with darkness because since we have seen it closely, we know we don't deserve to be here. We know that its something external and all we can do is to turn on the inner light of wisdom and get ourselves out of it.

However, often when we try to search for shortcuts to get outta our mess not realizing that it's a process, that we have to build through it and not run through it. There are no shortcuts to success and no 'cut, push jump' through darkness. We have to go deep into it, endure through it and that's when we can come out shining like an Empress. And after that, we are so powerful that darkness will not just 'not' tamper us, but it's afraid of us. So, how do we do all of this? The first step is to know what we deserve and we don't settle, we don't accept anything lesser than we deserve. This also means not settling for just the moon and the stars but going beyond and trying our luck through our hard-work for getting this entire galaxy. We know that we are meant for greater things so we heal ourselves and pick up our pieces to start walking towards light. We realise our power in every situation and the amount of power we have to limit giving to external conditions over us. We cut our losses and get things moving, we understand that it's not luck but just a phase which we will get through.

And self-pity? No, there's no such word in our dictionary, we make our dreams come true and above all odds we strive to the victory that's written in our fate. We become the empress that we are always meant to be and it may get cold sometimes on the throne but we never lose sight of our fire ???

# III

# The True love of your life ?

How you love yourself is How you
teach others to love you

Rupi Kaur


OurMindfulLife.com


*Everytime I see the mirror, I see the sunshine ?*

Remember when you're lost in the darkness..... look for the light... and when you search for the light, look within ?

'Oh this is what happens always. There is nothing new this time. I knew this would happen, it's the story of my life', then she took a sip again. This was my cousin who is in her dating phase again after a break-up and she wanted to go out drinking to 'forget her past'. As if the entire past would just go down in some drinks. I was trying to console her with the age-old 'he didn't deserve you, you can do so much better....'. She was hurt and she wanted to move on. She was swiping on her dating app and telling me how she could get any of these guys and how any guy would be lucky to have her. I was supporting her then trying to boost her ego and make her feel better.

Isn't that what all of us do. We get into relationships/situationships where we connect with the other person, we try to find a common ground of bonding and then we try to look for our happiness, stability and sense of belonging in 'our person'. Well, this drill is totally normal and its what all of us do until we find out that 'our person' is not so perfect or what we expect them to be or what we thought they would be like when *we put them in the 'my person' bracket.*

But I ask you, through this blog, to take a step back, go within yourself and ask why put so much load of expectations of what you want, what your happiness looks like on another person? And then go through the process of that relationship to find out that what you started it with is not what you are able to find in that relationship. It's not fair, neither to you nor the other person. Let's say you are expecting love from someone whose heart is closed, he or she is not capable of loving so its no use expecting love from them, but you still put that weight on them and get upset when you don't see that coming from them. My dear friend it's not them who upset you, because it's like you were asking a scientist about art or vice versa. Besides, if you were looking for love with a broken heart from a previous relationship, you were probably looking for a cushion to take away your pain and not a person to love.

All that said and done, the purpose of this blog is not to tell you to stop looking for love or to be miserable, but rather to find it in the right place, starting with your own heart. It is also to identify, when you should open your heart to somebody, and if they are really in that same place where they can reciprocate to make the relationship balanced. Well, I do believe that most of our miseries are self-inflicted and that we and only we have the power to get ourselves out of them. Maybe that person is not capable of love, maybe you still have some impending trust issues in every relationship, maybe you thought the person was what you were looking for, maybe the timing was not right, maybes that don't end leading you to a place of confusion. There is only one life and there is sooo much more to do than to spend your days in confusing emotions about your love life. Besides, there are so many people in your life who love you, trust you, value you, look up to you and are grateful for you. Every person is going through their own struggles so all that we can do is be kind to everyone but first of all be kind to ourselves.

So coming back to my cousin, she started going like — no more players, no more emotionally unavailable men, no more mixed signals, I am only going to look for kings, evolved, nurturing, caring and kind men. But I wanted to tell her, before jumping out from one broken relationship and getting into the 'safety pad' of another relationship on the pretext of finding stability and love through a certain stereotype of men, maybe introspect, change your expectations and become the version of yourself that you would fall in love with. If we don't become someone who we love, how can we expect others to see us as someone to be loved? So instead of going like — no more players, emotionally unavailable men.... Blah, why not go like — no more getting in my way, no more of not realising how wonderful I am, no more not seeing the amazing person in the mirror staring back at me and no more of not knowing that I deserve to be loved and respected without asking for it. Yes, when you know who you are and what you deserve, if you have to ask for people to see it, then maybe you are in the wrong place. Its like an artist who needs the right audience to understand his/her art.

So ladies and gentlemen, whoever you get into the next relationship with, always know that its you and only always you who is your one true love who has to realize your worth and also teach others how to love you the right way. Let your true love decide how to love you and make you goddamn happy ?♥?

# IV

# Like a star in the sky

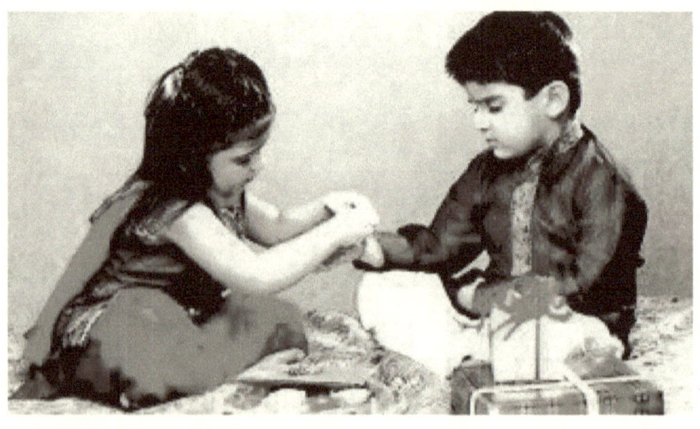

*Never apart, always in my heart*

Like a star in the sky you shine your light on us
Its that day again when your memories will haunt me
It's that memory again when every year you called me

I remember our last year's meeting when you didn't have a lot of time

You had to rush somewhere, I hesitated at first but then said its fine.

You had promised to protect me although you knew I didn't need protection

You were gonna be there but you broke our connection

I wish today would have been just like every year

When you would smile and have lunch with me

I wish I could still tie my Rakhi to your hand this year

And you would give some amazing rakhi gift to me

This year its different and we know you are missing

But to see you once again is all that I am wishing

Dear brother you are so far away and out of my sight

I can't forget your sweet dimples and your heartwarming smile

Somewhere in some far off other world realm

If you can still see and hear us

I hope you are able to see then

That we miss you and remember our every small moment

I know you are watching over us

And when we get sad you also cry

So today I am only going to smile

So that I can see you shine like a star in the sky

*Ps: We all miss you and love you but I know you smile when we smile... so here's to smiling our way through today and keeping you in our hearts forever and ever* ❤?❤?

# V

# The different faces of grief – An inspiring fact that I realised

*I didn't know what stuck until I faced it and shined brighter*

In the past few days I have seen death more frequently than I thought someone can in a year. Death came over us like a storm and it took away everything that was precious. We never realized what happened till we were faced with the dark claws of death and lost our person.

Grief, sadness, pain, overwhelming feelings of missing someone – Yes, we all have been through it many times in our lives, especially when we have lost someone for good. The first instinct that we get is, this is just temporary. 'No, they will be back, they have to be. We have been through so much, we'll go through this again and we'll evolve stronger.' Then we also say 'This is not true, they are not gone, I'll see them again tomorrow.' And then there is 'How can this happen? When did it happen? Why did I not prevent it? What could I have done better to prevent it from happening?

Grief mostly comes with questions – the what, why, how of everything that happened to cause us this grief. But none answered. The questions come to us as bullets that cause pain and leave us hanging in distress.

Grief comes uninvited and stays for longer than expected. We try to stop it, we try to hide it, we try to face it and then when we are truly healing, we try to embrace it. So when in grief, we all have our own ways of dealing with it. This blog talks about the different faces of grief and finally, how we try to overcome it.

First comes the scary face when grief strikes us and we don't want to look at it since its so scary. Our first instinct is to ignore it. We want to wipe it off and pretend that it never happened. Its scary to look at it. We are in denial, no won't give in to grief. But like a parasite, grief doesn't let us go. Grief keeps reminding us of its presence until we have no choice but to face it.

Okay, then bring it on. Lets face it head on. This is when we get into our fighter phase and grief gets into its poisonous face. It tries to push us back. It tries to dominate us, tries to weaken our rebellion. This is perhaps a very difficult phase for us. We need to keep fighting and reminding ourselves that we are stronger. If we are surrounded by our family and friends, this journey becomes easier. But I want to reach out to those who are not having someone to help them get through this phase – I wanna say that you are so much more stronger and wonderful than your fears and that you are not alone. You can get through this phase.

Once we get through this, grief still doesn't let us go. It now comes in the form of a victim. It tells us that how can we let go of the pain so easily. Aren't we supposed to hold on to it and cry some more? Did we really love our person if we can let go off the grief so early? Why don't we cry that often now? Does it mean that we have forgotten them? These are the questions that grief comes up with. And we do believe that these are reasonable questions. Yes, we should cry more and shed more tears. Why are we then getting to that point where it doesn't hurt so much that we cry? Its not like we never loved them. Infact, we loved them so much, we still do and will always do. But why isn't that showing through our tears? Because my friend, you have levelled up through the difficult phase and have faced your grief head on. Be proud and stand tall, we are moving on to the next phase.

So here we are in our next phase and now grief is like a child. It wants our attention but we are more mature now. We thank everything that happened to us which made us stronger. We lost some important people, but we know that they will be waiting on the other side for us to join them. We go to that place called healing. Our people are right there with us always guiding us like a shining star. Yes! Thats what they are. They are stars, shining so bright for us and giving us their light. Wouldn't wanna greet them now with a teary face? They are happy, smiling and all their happy memories are kept close to our hearts. 'Nope, we are never letting them go' – but we say this with a smile. A smile that gives us the strength to pick our life and also to pick our dear ones. We will walk through this phase with grief by our side wanting that attention that it will not get.

Enter, 'Your Phase'. We have been through so much, endured a lot many things and had to stop ourselves from breaking. We have walked through the darkness and now not a single bloody damn blackout can scare us. We are nocturnal, we have adjusted, we have endured, we have seen it all and we haven't broken, neither have we changed. We have become more wonderful. We are now one of a kind. We know our metal will not melt even with whatever life brings our way. We may have to face grief again but we know that we are well prepared. We have a lot of pain, so much pain that still stays with us but you know what??? We have turned more powerful through our pain. Pain is our reality and pain is what drives us to build ourselves. So my dear friends, grief is not here to break us, its a fact, a reality that is here to transform us. We will be faced with grief and pain again, but we only have to remember, that every little step towards this pain, is only going to make us shine brighter like our people who are now stars, who will be watching us from above and smiling when we win in all phases of life!♥?

# VI

## Till we meet again...

*The bond that will always shine within me*

I know that I lost you
I also know that you had to go
I know you were trying
But you could not show
   I tried to bring you back
I tried to end your pain
I knew you wanted to come home
I knew you wanted to, but you were ashamed
   I wish I could go back to that moment
When things got out of control
I wish I could make it all right
And bring you back home
   I can feel how difficult it must have been for you
To be getting over your demons
You were showing the world a face
But slowly you were fading away
   Beneath the mask of pride
Beneath all the fake prologues
Beneath the yearning for respect
You just wanted some love
   I wish you had opened up more
And told me what was bothering you then
I wish you had let your heart out
And didn't play pretend
   If it were for me
I would have kept you safe
If I could have one wish
I would have let things reshape
   Now you are far away
I hope you are at peace anyway

We will always miss you
And hope you return back someday
    Dearest brother – I just wanted to say
That I love you and will always remember you
Till I meet my grave and till we meet again

# VII

# Focus on the sunshine

*They may be powerful, but they are not the sun, you are!*

Another blog post to try and motivate you? To help you get through whatever it is that makes your life difficult? Nope, no blog or motivational quotes can get you out of sadness (although I think that music can, cuz music is very powerful), but we all have to work through our own shadows to make our life better. Blogs, motivational quotes, speeches are all catalysts for us to take action and come out of that dark place. This blog is just another one of the many catalysts to make you help yourself. I hope it is able to serve the purpose for which it is designed. Now I don't want to go on saying that you can do it, that you need to keep fighting and that you can be strong and get over it.

On the contrary, I would say that you need to face that sadness. Don't be strong or tough 'it is time to be vulnerable, to be open to face your fears, to be weak, to cry and accept that you are not extra ordinary but a normal person who needs to let their emotions come out and help you start your healing journey. Have you ever wondered that most times when we are sad, and if we try to share it with our family or friends, they try to cheer us up. They try to lift our mood and as good friends that they are, they tell us to forget the past and move on. Well, they care about us and want us to be happy again, but is forgetting the past and moving on the best advice? It is like closing the lid to an open jar of memories. You can close the lid now, but if by any chance the lid reopens again, the contents inside the jar are in fact giving the same energy, that same fragrance and those same moments that we lived. Now, if they are happy memories, I'd say go for a whiff or a scent but what if these are painful moments? Do you really want to then keep the lid always a bit open to expose the contents inside. Why would you want that, of course not? Why would anyone want that? So, while you read further on to this blog, go on empty that jar and tightly close the lid to all the past hurt and pain. Then come back and listen to what am about to say.

Well, that was unreasonable of me right? But that's how normally life wants us to be like. Like, okay you are going through this pain and hurt and all but you have to keep moving on cuz as life am not gonna wait for you, that's normally the overall message that life keeps giving us. Aaandd we have no choice but to oblige. Or do we? Well, yes we do. We have the choice to open those wounds, spare a minute and address the pain. Cuz if we don't now, we'll again leave the lid half closed with those painful memories and one small little setback is gonna make the jar open up and that pain is gonna stare right back at us. So why not address it right now, deal with it and close it tightly. You don't need to be strong, don't need to show the world that you are tough or mature. It's okay to be vulnerable and be sad for a minute so that you can heal and really be happy not just on paper but in reality. You deserve this happiness and you and only you can give it to yourself. Breath in your pain and breathe out your darkness, only keep that part of your pain which tells you that you have gone through this already, that it has transformed you not into a more stronger version of yourself but a more open, loving and kind version of yourself, that you'll think twice before hurting someone cuz you have been there and that now, you only need to focus on the sunshine honey!! ❤??

# VIII

It's the choices that make us who we are? Or do they?

*Growth is not measured, it is lived!*

Yes, we have heard this quote and yes it is so true. Then what is this blog about? It is exactly what the title says – The choices that make us. Perhaps we underestimate the power of choices. These choices make us who we are and this is so true, it's actually tried and tested true. Now lets get into the blog. Have you ever wondered why sometimes even when we make the right choice it may later turn out to be a wrong one? Does that mean we don't know how to make the right choice? Nope, it only means that we are getting nearer to becoming the best judge of what really matters to us even if it means that it may not be seeming like the right choice at the moment. Well, that said, we are sometimes faced with very difficult choices. There may be no right choice and sometimes we are not left with any choice.

Actually, I want to go deeper into the last line. Do we really have no choice or do we choose to ignore our choices and play the victim. I think 9 out of 10 times its the latter. We play victim and say, I'm sorry I couldn't get a decent job because I had to support my home so I took the first job that I came across. I couldn't be with the love of my life because she/he did not reciprocate. We never say that I did not try beyond that first obstacle of my family problems to look for a better job. That because the person I liked did not reciprocate, I concluded that my love life is doomed. What we actually should know is we never tried again to get a better job, to take responsibility of our life and our problems and try and find a solution, that we never even told the person we liked of what a good life we can have together. We just blame it on our bad luck and take the easy way out. Instead of trying to change our life, we blame it either on the situation or another person and not look at the fact that we always had a choice to make our life better.

Okay, so now we know that we always had a choice, always have a choice. But what if sometimes we have many choices? Sometimes we are spoilt for choices. Sometimes we have so many choices that we don't know who or what to choose. That out of so many choices, which is that one choice that will actually be the right one for me. Now most times we would face this in simple things of life like choosing an outfit to wear for an evening or what to order in a restaurant or a perfect holiday spot. But there are times when these choices are put to us in life changing events – to select a perfect guy or girl, to select a study stream, to select the perfect university. How do we then select the best choice? These are the choices that make or break us so we need to make the right choice. In these type of situation, we need to assess what is that one choice that has the capacity to be the most influential in our life. Who is that one person who dims the light of all the other people I have known and speaks to my heart. And do I know that he/she will go to the end of this world to be with me? Now you may say that while I know that this person speaks to my heart, how can I say what their actions towards me would be, that they will go to the end of world to be with me? Well, here I would say that you need to look at the person beyond your lens of the association you've had with them. Are they a loyal person generally? Do they keep their promises if not to others, at least to themselves? Look at what their actions try to tell you. Are they indecisive about many things? Hot and cold in other relationships of their life? Do any of their general characteristics give a big green flag that they will go to the end of the world for the things they love? Unless you don't see these green flags, no matter how much your heart speaks their language,they are not your person.

If they are a toxic person, chances are they will bring their toxicity to the relationship. If they are hot and cold, in and out or in general indecisive, a relationship with you is not going to change that. So we need to be very careful when we are making these important choices. But as humans, our choices become biased based on some experience we might have had with the specific person/ relationship/ university study stream. We do not think that outside of our lens of likeability, outside of our relationship, the guy or the girl we so wanna spend our life with maybe a different person. Then maybe we realise this when reality of everyday life, responsibilities and other relationships start flowing in. We see their general behaviours and feel that they have changed. Now that isn't fair, is it? Its like you are telling a fish that they weren't swimming earlier and they started that after few years of relationship with you? No my friend, he was always the swimmer. That guy/girl who didn't treat you well may not have been the best at relationships. So it is very important to know that when we make these choices, we look at them through unbiased lens. Also instead of blaming the other person, realise that you did not do your homework before making that important decision of your life.

Okay these are situations that are under your control where you have a choice to make. But what about those situations where you are one of the many choices that a person has to make? Imagine you have told someone your feelings and they, instead of giving a firm answer to you, whether they wanna be with you or not, are unable to decide. He/she can't decide between you and another person or He/she can't decide if they want to be with you or be single. What do you do in that case? You may think that it is their choice and they are yet to make their final choice. Well, if you ask me, by not making a choice they are actually making a choice. Not choosing if they want you or not is a choice of not choosing you. So do not waste your time running behind a miracle or an illusion that someday they might choose you. Anyone who wants to be with you in true sense will actually 'go to the ends of the world' to make it happen, period, and if you remain stuck in that situation, it is a choice you made so do not blame anyone else for wasting your time. Then again, there are situations when people love someone but they choose ignoring it over expressing those feelings. Every inaction is also a choice to not proceed with the situation.

So, to conclude this ' longer than intended to be' post, do choices make us who we are? Yes, they do but only when they turn into decisions. Cuz, we may be able to go back to our choices, but when they turn into decisions, that is what makes or breaks our situations. Choices are made but decisions, decisions are owned. You need to live by them.

So when making these choices, think 2 steps ahead for how they will look when they turn into life changing decisions cuz it's these decisions that are gonna make you who you are, they can make you happy and awesome ♥?

# IX

Read this for when you wonder: Why did it happen to me?

*Challenges came to me, so that they can sharpen my edges!*

So after a long time I decided to write this post. I mean I can't time them and write them. I write them when a thought comes to my mind and I want to pen it down or feel like it's worthwhile sharing with the world. And today's thought I feel is very much worthwhile sharing with everyone. I know that I am not a very popular writer and that some of you may not even like what I write. But if through my blogs, even a single person is inspired or it makes a difference to his/her perspective, then it's worth the read.

I think this was a random epiphany that I got on a random day doing some random deep thinking. It makes me wonder, how the Universe has its own way of doing things or rather, might I say, making things work for us. Ever wondered why you never got that job or that girl/guy? Why did you sometimes felt that all the worse things are happening together? Why everytime you are at the short end of the stick? And then it makes you think that there is some associated bad luck or bad karma which is playing out for you in the worst possible ways. While I do believe in karma, not everything bad that happens to us is karmic.

Okay, so when our situations get really 'screwed up' and it's not karmic, what is it? I was recently having a conversation with my cousin who was going through a situation when this came up. She said that she never harmed anyone, never intentionally hurt anyone, never intended bad for anyone then 'why did this happen to me?'

That's when I asked this question out loud to myself and to her – Why did it happen to her? Was it to give her a taste of bad karma? Or was it to give her a lesson she won't forget? Keeping aside the situation she was going through, there was something else that we realised then. It's always the bad that happens to us where we find something external of ourselves to put the blame on. I mean if we think about it, how many times have you thought that when you got a job raise – Why did this happen to me? Or when you got that perfect proposal, did you think of why did it happen to you? We didn't, I didnt, she didn't. We don't do that. We never question the reasons behind the good things that happen to us or put out the blame externally. Sometimes maybe we just say that it could be a result of the good karma but most times when good things happen to us, we always say that it was a result of our hardwork, effort, energy and time. We got that job/money because we manifested abundance. We got that proposal because our energy shifted from being self pitying to being confident in ourselves. We started loving ourselves and that's when love came to us.

Now about the bad stuff that happened to us, was it something we manifested? Maybe or maybe not, that's not something which we would know. But we sure know one thing – Every bad thing that happens or happened to us does not have to have a reason external to us. It only means that this is the time when we have to go inside ourselves, assess our situation, understand our inner strength and come out to face it and more so to change it, because if it's happened to us, it means we can endure it. So tomorrow when something bad happens, instead of saying – 'Why did this happened to us?', we'd rather say – 'If this has happened, it means we can fix it? So when do we begin?' ♥??

# X

# In the web of relationships and love... Where are 'You'?

*I am not defined by a relationship, I am abstract being in
my own state of art!*

So I am confident that this blog is going to help most
of my friends out there. I was recently in discussion with
a friend of mine who was facing some issues in her
relationship with her husband. She felt like her husband
didn't care for her and while he would say many things, he
didn't show it through his actions.

I wanted to tell her what was the right thing to do
without trying to break her marriage but I too got a little
emotional and offended by her husband's behaviour.
Maybe because I have seen this type of behaviour before
in some of my other friends' relationships. Also maybe
because I realised that these things still trigger me. That was
also when I realised that I myself am not completely healed
from my past wounds. Maybe we don't heal as easily from

our wounds.

Sometimes we do a lot of work on ourselves and it only takes one moment, one action, that resembles our past experiences to trigger us and leads us back to the person we were when we had those fresh wounds. And then all the old wounds are open and we realise – I need to heal more.

And while theoretically we are much wiser, much happier, much knowing of how to handle such situations.. we can't bring it to action when faced with the same events that occurred in our past. If someone has hurt you in the past by being closed off to your love (like in my friends case), when you again venture into the land of relationships and see that there is another one who is again closed off, you immediately back off and run to the other direction. Actually my friends, this doesn't mean that you are not healed, it only means that you are human. Our brain remembers what happened to us in these type of situations and immediately decides a Plan A and Plan B.

So this would probably be your brain at the time:

Plan A : make the other person feel comfortable and let him/her open up to you. But you did this the last time and look where it got you. So let's go with Plan B

Plan B: Close off, run away, don't you be vulnerable, act cool, don't care, indulge somewhere else.

Yeah, we all might have done this at some point and that is what makes us humans. We always tend to protect ourselves, sometimes from people, conversations and most times from our own emotions. We don't want to be thought of as the emotional ones, the needy ones, the vulnerable ones because that makes us look like we are dependent on the other person for our happiness. To tell you honestly, being vulnerable for someone doesn't make you dependent on them for your happiness, that is only what the other person thinks of you.

So when you show your emotions to someone, you make them feel important.. the other person might feel you are happy because of them, but that is not true. If you feel that you are happy because of them, it is their opinion of your relationship and not yours. Don't let someone else's opinion blur your own thoughts about your happiness. You are happy because you feel those amazing emotions within yourself, because now you can share them with someone other than yourselves and because you have the liberty to express your emotions and experience yourself as a person. When you try to see yourself from someone else's opinion, that's when you feel that you are happy because of the other person. No my friend, you are happy because you experienced a different side of you, because you realised how amazingly loving you can be, how beautiful you look when you are vulnerable. That is what should make you happy.

So I spoke about us being humans. Many times we say we learnt from the past. But yet, we hurt again by repeating the same things we did in our past. Have you ever seen yourself repeating the same patterns in all of your relationships? Even knowing that some of them have broken your past relationships. If yes, then do you think you have learnt nothing from your past? Well, that is not true. Experiences alert us but they can't completely change us as a person. So if you are an emotional person, you will still be an emotional person. Maybe 8 times out of 10 you will be closed off but there will be those 2 times when the dam breaks and your emotions are all over the place.

So it's okay if some things trigger you and take you back to the place/person from where you started to evolve. We can go back to square one but it's important for us to know that we don't *belong to square one.* I may get triggered and may go back to being what I was in the past as long as I know that that's not the place where I belong, where I can stay and that I gotta start the work to get back to the 'evolved me' version of myself.

And then how do we do that... By looking for solace in another relationship? By trying to indulge ourselves in substances? By trying to keep busy and act cool? Nope... we do that just by putting our complete honest faith and growth plans in the one person who has always been with us, always helped us change, always driven us and have been our hero – Our own self ♥??

# XI

# How I connected the Gita and Shiv Vani

*He is the ultimate guide to all our life questions*

So this post I think is one of my most thought over post on two of the most religious books based on teachings of Shri Krishna and my fav god Mahadev. Being a Mahadev bhakt, I initially tend to be more inclined towards Shiv Vani and it's impact on me and my life. The way it changed my thought process and my perspective towards life. Although to be very honest, Shiv Vani is so vast that it cannot be explained in a small blog. Honestly, Shiv Vani is like that a vast ocean which is a never ending source of knowledge. The knowledge that is the solution to all our problems. The knowledge to lead the ship of your life. The knowledge that when combined with 'Srimad Bhagvad Gita' herein referred to as 'The Gita', completely transforms you as a person. The way one can relate to the teachings of these two books and apply it to practical usage can bring amazing changes in life. So firstly let us look at some small extracts of these books

### 'Stit Pragya' in The Gita:

The Gita states that a person has to be grounded, balanced and rooted to his/her core no matter whatever happens in his/her external environment. Imagine a river – it is very flowing, it changes its boundaries when small creek water enters the river, when the climate changes or when there is some external changes in the environment. The river flow also depends on the flow of the wind and rainfall. The higher the rainfall, the more unstable is the river. The Gita states, that a person should not be like a river who becomes unstable with small changes in his/her external environment. A person should be like an ocean in which all rivers ultimately flow in and make it more deeper without changing its stability. A person should be like that rock on the sea shore where no matter how many waves crash, they cannot shake the rock.

Now, I know it is very difficult to attain this level of internal emotional balance and stability, but when you hear what the Shiv vani says, you can see the road to achieve this, maybe not completely but partially atleast. The Shiv Vani says, anything external of you that tries to deter you or your stability, is, in itself not stable. So if something or someone tries to stress you out by showing lack of compassion or trying to demean you or behave in a certain way which will trigger you, know that it is the nature of that person and has nothing to do with you. The greatest power that one can have is to be calm and non-reactive when someone criticizes you. How to do this? Well, by just knowing that the criticism is that other person's opinion of you and not the facts about you. When you accept their opinion to be the facts about you, that's when you are triggered. For Eg: If someone criticizes you as being blind, you don't take it personally because you can physically see and the fact is that you are not blind (FYI, being blind is still not a criticism, it enhances your other senses). However, if you are short and someone calls you short, you will take it personally because that is a fact about you. But then, if it is your reality, so be it… accept your reality and there is nothing to be ashamed about it.

Its a very deep form of explanation that Shiv Vani gives you on how to be stable and non-reactive to triggering situations. I can't explain its vastness in this small blog. But just know that learning the mysteries of life from Gita and their application from Shiv Vani will really balance you out as a person and make you content.

### <u>'Karma Chakra' in The Gita</u>

We all know about the famous saying – Just do your karma and do not worry about the results. When Arjun was hesitant to kill the people of his own kin during the war stating that he didn't want to be a murderer, Lord Shri Krishna reminded him of who he was and what was his Karma. His guidance said that one should just do his karma and not worry about what are the results. Do you Karma and let the results be in the hands of god. So if you want something in your life, just do the work that is needed to get closer to your results and do not keep any expectations of whether the results will be in your favour or not. If your efforts are true, your results will also be positive. Just keep the faith and keep doing your karma.

Shiv Vani goes a step beyond the Karma Chakra. It says, Do your karma, do not expect any results but don't do karma just for your results. Do not do karma just for you. Now that you are fulfilled in your life and can fill your cup of abundance, do karma that will help others to be abundant. Shiv Vani says, do your karma not to balance your karma, do your karma because that is the purpose of your life. Once you have fulfilled yourself, then do more karma which will help those around you, outside of you.

Well, if I take these small percepts from The Gita and match it with the Shiv Vani concepts, it would create a book probably titled 'How to be always always happy, stable and abundant in life'. Most of our life problems are resolved in these books and they can really give us some great guidance on how to solve your problems and live the most amazing stable life.

Today's blog was just a humble attempt from my side to give a little know how on what these books have taught me and how my Shiva inspires and lives in my perception of life. Being with Shiva does not mean I need to dress a certain way, look a certain way, smoke a certain way or dance a certain way, being with Shiva for me means to get beyond myself and knowing him within me. May you also find the light of Shiva within you and may it take away all your worries. Om Namah Shivay??

# XII

# How to heal yourself, be grounded and remain grounded

*Healing is neither a science, nor an art, healing is a form of meditation!*

You might have read so many articles on healing. Maybe on how crystals can help you relax, meditation will lead you to calmness and rituals can help you cleanse your energy. While, some of them may help you, I wanted to share this article too which may help you further in your healing journey.

So let's start from the beginning, when you were wounded. I know that the times that you have been through have not been easy. That you had to face so many challenges and also had to face your inner demons. It's easy to face what the outside world brings on to you but when you have to face yourself internally, your inner demons and get to terms with the way it impacts the people around you, trust me it gets very very difficult and this is your first step to being your amazing self. I think when you take this step, you should start to be proud of yourself. Now we all have been through those times. Through the difficult times which shape us in a certain way. Some childhood issues, some broken hearts, some bad memories, some abuses which make us who we are today. It's because we are like a bottle that takes all these life experiences within us and adjust our temperament to these challenges. We tend to keep them close to our heart so that they can act as a shield and protect us from getting heart broken again, facing our issues again, reliving those bad memories and abuses again.

We try to let these past challenges, problems and issues to guard our future expectations and experiences. Because, we don't want to fall in that same trap again. Let me give a small example: Sometimes, people who are wounded in love, will have multiple partners. They will consciously avoid getting into a stable serious relationship because they want to protect themselves from another heart break

Life goes on and we get used to living our lives with this guard on our hearts. We don't open up. We live in our shelves. We never give a chance to our future because we are stuck on what happened to us in the past and slowly without our knowing, our present which could have been so much more beautiful becomes a past memory of a time when we feared to open our hearts to the beautiful moments of life.

And then we say, nothing good happens to us. My dear friends, the good is just waiting to happen to you only if you allow it to happen. I know it was difficult for you in the past and I understand why you want to protect yourself now. But if you never try to open up, never try to let people in, to allow experiences to happen, to allow 'mistakes' to happen, how will you ever grow and be happy again, or make new memories if you are still stuck on the past painful moments?

Stop being on this cycle of the same sad memories of the past, let go what happened to you in your childhood. I know it was difficult for you and that's exactly why you deserve to happy with new sweet memories in your life. Let life happen to you. You have given so many chances to these past sad memories, now give a chance to healing them. You deserve this healing.

One way which might help you to heal is by healing others. When you start to look at other peoples sadness not just from the outside but from the inside, meaning when you start to feel how they feel, your sadness starts to leave you. You realize that you are not alone in that place. It gives you strength, the strength to carry someone, to provide for someone, to nurture and care for someone and it helps you forget your wounds. It also makes you grounded. You start to understand that you have been through difficult times but so have others and maybe their difficult times have been far more challenging than yours. This then leads to the realisation that you are fortunate and should have gratitude for what you have in life. Yes, your life has not been perfect, but if you try and give a chance to your healing, it wouldn't be less than a dream come true ♥?

I am not a healing counsellor or an expert but I know that when I started to look at other people's wounds and started to heal them, my own wounds vanished. I can't fuss up in my own mess when I have people to take care of and when I started loving and caring for them, I started loving myself.

Sometimes people confuse self love with pride. Loving yourself does not mean that others are not be loved. Yes, you are special but so are all those other people in your life who give you memories good or bad. Once you understand this, you will become grounded. Time is the biggest reason to be grounded and a reminder that nothing is permanent. If you are beautiful, it will fade someday, if you are rich, your fortune can change in a day, if you are powerful, you can be stripped of that someday. What will remain is your kind heart, your loving self, your empathetic nature and the fire within you to make the best of your life and give an amazing life to those around you ♥?♥?

# XIII

If you are an Empath, this is for you ♥? If you are not an Empath, then this is definitely for you ♥?

*Empaths are rare, if you are one, cherish yourself!*

Okay, before I start with my post, am sure by now you all would know who or what is an Empath and also whether you are one of them or not. To tell you in short, an Empath is a person who feels what you feel, who knows how you feel it, who is very very intuitive, who can feel through your pain and sorrow and who absorbs all of it and turns it into something happy for you. Being an Empath is exhausting and being around one is enlightening.

So if you are an Empath, congratulations for being some of most powerful people we have and if you have an Empath around you, then consider yourselves blessed. So let me tell you what is the hype about Empathy.

When we started off as children, we were taught some things – like we should not lie, steal, hurt others, disrespect people, make fun of someone or be violent. But the problem is no one told us why we shouldn't do all these things. Why should I not steal? Just because it's bad, no... because stealing from someone will create a lack for that other person who might have some emotional value to the things we steal or who might face some problems due to our stealing from them. While lying is not a good thing but does it mean that we shouldn't lie if it makes someone else happy? Hurting someone is a bad thing because? Do you get my point, our slate was blank if someone would ask why these things are bad, and we being the obedient children never asked anyone the reasons for these things being labelled as 'bad'. So naturally we didn't learn to be empathetic since our childhood.

However, our very core of empathy begins here. We didn't steal because it's bad, we were also taught that it will create bad karma for us and hence we shouldn't do it. I mean, that is so selfish. My mom, am so proud of her, always told me the reasons for not doing bad things. Yes when I was very very small to understand anything, she told me that lying or stealing would make a monster jump in my bed at night. But as I grew older, she told me to think from the perspective that if that same thing happened to me, how would I feel. She told me to open up my thoughts and think from the other side. She was the first Empath that I met.

So when you do something good for others, why do you do that? Is the reason selfish? Do you want to balance your karma? Or do you want to make yourself feel good about it? What part in this does the other person who you are doing good to plays? Isn't it selfish to do something good for someone so that you can get good karma? Or to make someone happy so that it gives you peace? Yes it is, but don't sooo many of us have these reasons to do good things for others? Yes, that's why empathy is a big deal

Empaths don't do good things to make themselves happy, peaceful or get good karma. Empaths do good things because they feel your pain, they can see through your eyes and they can know how you would be feeling to go through that pain and they try to lift you up by saying some good things or doing some good things for you. That's how Empaths attract so many sad, lonely, depressed people to them.

Sympathy is easy to be found, but empathy is very rare. When you do something for someone because you want to feel good about yourself, for eg: I'll give him food because I already have so much to eat and thankfully have been very blessed and lucky in life so I need to give food to the less fortunate- this is Sympathy.

And when you say, I'll give him food because he hasn't eaten in so many days, he will get weak and will lose that small chance to have a life and an opportunity to change his circumstances- this is Empathy.

Empathy is rare and only an Empath knows how difficult it is to get someone who understands him/her. But even then he/she doesn't expect someone to misbalance themselves and understand him/her. Empath is someone who is so strong in himself/herself that he/she can take the weight of others and help them grow. Empathy is that water to help grow the plant. Empathy is like the roof of the house that takes in all the heat to keep those within them cooler. Empathy is rare but so much more needed. Empathy is one of the most powerful and strong traits a person can have. When you feel someone and help them grow, you have to know that you are so full of light that it vanishes the darkness of everyone who comes in your life.

Mother, is the symbol of an Empath for her child. Empathy is selfless, unique, loving and so much needed in our world. My dear Empaths, I know the weight that you carry to bring light into the darkness and to uplift and grow others is tremendous and it's exhausting for you. Just know that you are the so very brave, powerful and required in our world. Ain't no one as strong as you are. My dear readers, you can find anyone you want but if you have an Empath in your life, hold them tight and keep learning from them.

Thank you mom, for being the first Empath of my life. I hope I learn from your shine and light the lives of those around me. I love you ♥?♥?

# XIV

# What are you made of?

*Its not what around you but whats within you that matters!*

Maybe you will not agree with this post, maybe you will. But then again, everyone has their own opinion. Today's post is written by me through some live examples of people around me that I have seen throughout my childhood. I have met diverse type of people since my childhood and each of their stories are different and unique in their own way. But one thing was common in all their stories – each one was made by circumstances and choices. They had their own circumstances and they made their own choices. Sometimes good, sometimes very bad and sometimes, uncontrollable.

Do you know about that saying we hear so many times? Life does not happen to you, it happens for you and through you. Well, the more this type of life happens to you, the better you grow as a person. I think most times when we face challenges, we try to think that all the difficult times are meant for us. No no my friend, difficult times happen to make you stronger. They do happen to test your metal and make you even more stronger. It's like when you sail through the storm, you truly become the captain of your ship. And once a captain, always a captain man ?

Okay, so let me not tell you just big phrases and shed some light on the actual topic. For example, let us look at poverty. A person who is poor, not so well to do is automatically treated in a certain way by the society. He/she has to stand everywhere in queues, is given the last preference, has to listen to rich people's demands, has to struggle to achieve everything and after all this, he is still judged as being poor, lower class and most times people think they are not literate enough. Let's take another example, a prostitute. Immediately we judge her to be someone who is scandalous to be around, who may have an std, who shouldn't be befriended by the respectable people of the society. She is like an outcast from the society who is not supposed to mingle during day time and should be limited to being present in the nighttime and only at selective places. Another example is that of a person who has committed many crimes. Well, many times people are scared of him/her. Some of them have their own reasons to do the crimes and for some, it's just a way of life. The same thing applies to an alcoholic. Most times, we tend to judge an alcoholic with being a person who is good for nothing, someone who just doesn't care about his/her life and those around him/her, someone who is not responsible and doesn't think straight. And we all like balanced people, people whose head is in the right place and those who are responsible to not do any irrational actions.

Okay, now let's look at all these examples. If you'd have met the poor person before he/she became poor.. or the prostitute before she had to face some circumstances which led her to be a prostitute, wouldn't they be treated by you equally as any other person of your 'society'? Her kids would be going in the same school as your kids did, lived in the same area as you live, hang around the same places as you do. What am trying to say is that when you are treating these people, you are not looking at the person, you are only looking at the label that some not so kind circumstances has led that person to be where they are in their life. What if the same circumstances happened to you? Would you still look at her the same way? Or treat her the same? I don't think so.

Let's talk about the other example. There is definitely nothing to talk about criminals but while I empathise to some extent with alcoholics, I feel that the people who fall in the criminal/ alcoholic category are someone who are made by their choices. It's not their circumstances that made them who they are. Well, to some extent circumstances did play a role but the choice was made by them. They could've chosen to be different, do different and think differently but they chose not to do so.

The circumstances that happen to us decide for us but it's the choices that we make that define us. If you are a prostitute made by her circumstances, if you were born in a poor family, I'd still feel there is nothing that you should be ashamed of. You are trying your best to face your circumstances and live the life that you are given. You are brave and I respect that.

If you are an alcoholic pushed to the bottle due to your debt, money, girl, family problems, you always have the choice to change your circumstances.

So next time before you judge a person just think about what is it about him/her that is different from you. Is it his circumstances or his choices? What is it that he is made of? And if you'd been in his place, what would you be made of? Your choices? Your circumstances? Or your strength?

# XV

# Ram Navmi special – What Ramayan teaches us

*When I search for the light, I see you!*

According to Maharshi Valmiki, today at 12 PM was the birth of Lord Ram at Ayodhya. After many years of asking for a child, god blessed King Dashrath and his wives with children. The oldest wife, Kaushalya gave birth to Lord Ram. Then started the story of Ramayana which shows how Lord Ram rescued his wife Sita from the clutches of Ravana and restored peace in his kingdom. There are some parts of Ramayan, that maybe written in black and white but are actually grey areas meant for us to think further.

For example, the story of Maharani Kai kai. She is shown as the cruel step mother of Rama who for her selfish reasons led him to go and stay in a forest with his newly wed wife, so that her son can sit on the throne. I think at the time when it was written, it was shown as such a huge sin done by Kai Kai. But tell me something, in today's world if you hear a mother doing that for her child, would you be surprised? Ofcourse it was wrong on her part to take away someone's right to throne and give it to her child. But what we called a sin then, becomes practicality in today's world. And if this would have happened in today's world, we would have called the guy who leaves his property for his step mother's word as either a 'saint' or a 'fool'. Let's look at the next character here, Laxman. The devoted brother left his life, his world and his wife to come and stay with his brother and sister-in-law in a forest. Was being a good brother his only responsibility? Wasn't he responsible to his wife and kids? Isn't Bharat, who took care of the kingdom in absence of his brother, fulfilling a higher duty towards not just his brother, but also all the people of the kingdom? Maybe it is written as black and white to show the representation of each of these characters individually. But the deeper meaning that it has is to understanding that the human mind and relationships are much more complex, atleast in today's 'Yug'

One of the main antagonist in the story is Ravan. That guy who became so obsessed with a beautiful woman that he went ahead and decided to kidnap her. His intention actually was to marry her, ofcourse for superficial reasons.

Of course then we have Lord Ram, who is the main protagonist of the story. Lord Ram, one of the avatars of Lord Vishnu. The ayodhya prince, the righteous one, the god in mans form who leads us all to light. He is the representation of all things good, the values, the roots, the ideal son, the ideal brother, the righteous king. But what about being the ideal husband? Did he fulfill that role completely. If yes, then why did he ask his wife for an 'Agni pariksha'? And what about Sita? Why is being the ideal, suffering wife her only role in the story? Maybe if we think further on this, when Ramayana happened, the world was more white and black the human emotions were not so complex. There were clear representations of good and bad traits that each of the individuals represented.

What I personally think is that Ramayana is not about just good vs. bad, black vs. white, Lord Ram vs. Ravana, god vs. evil. It goes beyond just this. It is a representation of all the human emotions and choices that we make which then decide our role in our story and the stories of the ones around us. Ofcourse selfishness is not the only trait that kai kai had, or desire for a woman is not the only characteristics of Ravana. There would definitely be more to their story. We all have some Kai Kai and Ravan within us. We have been Sita, Laxman, Ravan, Kai kai, Maharaj Dashrath and Lord Ram as well many times in our life.

What Ramayan wanted to tell us is that, there would be times and situations when we will have to deal with each of our inner traits that these characters represent. So before we judge someone to be a Ravan, we should try to look at the Ram within him/her. Because there would be times when we too may become selfish, obsessed, foolish, blinded, pitiful and sad. There would be times when we may be the Ravan in our story. We always have to remember that it doesn't make us bad, we have our situations which lead us to become the Ravan but it is very important for us to be a Ravan, to truly understand what it means to become Ram. The bad traits are very important for us to realise how good we can be. The true potential of the 'Ram' within us is only brought out when we have crossed the line of going through our Ravan (our demons) and finally, truly, found ourselves!

JAI SHREE RAM!!

Ps: I didn't mention my favourite Lord Hanuman (an avtar of Mahadev) but he is still always in my heart ♥?

*The views on this post are purely individual and independent of any religious beliefs. The post by no means intended to offend anyone or any religious beliefs*

# XVI

## Mamma's Boy

*A mother's love defines the man, makes the man !*

Just recently, I was talking to a friend of mine. We started with her saying that my birthday is coming up and what surprise am I gonna plan for the birthday. She wanted to wish me a day before my birthday since she was going to fly abroad the next day and would be in transit.

We have been very good friends since a long time and we caught up after a very long time. After the initial conversation about work, life and routine, we came to the topic of relationships. She had recently started a relationship and was saying that already she was not feeling the spark. She was saying that the relationship was not moving as per how she wanted it to go. She was saying that her partner was not what she had expected. I asked her what was the problem, what was she expecting that he wasn't able to give her. She said that he was very nice and sweet but he was a 'Mamma's Boy'. When I asked her what is the meaning of a 'Mamma's boy' for her, she said that he often talks to his mom, visits her, talks about how amazing she is and how he would like to stay with her for the entire life. She felt like he was comparing her to his mother and that someday he would expect her to do the same things as his mother does for him – like ironing his clothes, bringing him breakfast to his table, giving him his socks, keeping his files/laptop/lunchbox in his bag, giving him his towel while in the shower, putting up with all his tantrums and spoiling him.

Well, these things if done in relationships should be self inflicted and not to be requested. If you are in a relationship with someone, you can give him/her breakfast, make his/her stuff ready for when they leave for office and nurture them with your love and care all the time. But all these things should be felt from within and not forced on someone or expected from someone. I'll give you breakfast because I want to give you breakfast not because you asked me to do so. And trust me when I say that, if a woman is really in love with you, she treats you like her child. That's a natural motherly instinct that all women have towards the people they love. We protect them, care for them, nurture them, provide for them and treat them like our children. Can't help it, its just how we are designed. Don't be surprised if she starts talking to you like a child, taking care of all your needs, spoils you with new dishes to eat and you start crying in front of her, you feel protected and know that she will endure everything for you. Its like how a child feels in the care of his mother. So if you really want to understand what she feels for you, observe the way she treats you. Sometimes, its so complex to understand her love, because she might treat you like her child but that doesn't mean that she thinks you are a child. She respects you equally.

So if we are naturally motherly towards our partners, why are we scared of the mamma's boy type of guys? If you think about it deeply, maybe its not the 'mamma' that is the problem but the 'boy' that is the problem here. A person who is dependent on his partner for his daily needs like shoes, socks, clothes, files is not a grown up person. Doesn't matter if its a boy or a girl, if you need someone to keep your routine in place for you, you need to grow up and be self dependent. If you can't keep your clothes ready, socks in place and need someone to do these things for you – you are a boy or a girl yet to be transformed into a man or a woman. And boys or girls cannot withstand the huge amount responsibilities that come with a relationship. Sometimes, people are self reliant in the routine but are emotionally child like.

Emotional maturity is when you realize that the people who you love have their own needs, wants, desires and sometimes you may not always like their wants, needs or desires.

Ofcourse we must try to protect our people from going on the wrong path or somewhere we know would be destructive for them, but we have to respect their needs, wants, desires and understand when to let them live their life. It may not be necessary that your thoughts would always match or that he won't be dependent on you or that he will not be a little spoilt. But that's only because he was raised by a woman who cared for him, nurtured him and loved him very much when he was a boy and still does. Now, you may think that a mama's boy would also be someone who always sides with his mother in an argument, but I think a mama's boy really is the person that a guy becomes due to the influence of his mother on him. So a huge part of this depends on the mother and ofcourse a lot more also depends on the circumstances in which he grew and the people around him that designed his thoughts. If he never grew out of that phase of being a boy, you will get a child who needs to be taken care of his every need. But if he truly grew under the care of his mother and became a man with the roots of her values, then my dear ladies, this 'mama's boy' is the best thing that could happen to you ?

*PS: Someday, you would also be a mother to maybe a boy. Whether your child remains a boy or grows into a man, really does depend on you. If he really grows into the man of substance, then you would be proud someday looking at your 'mama's boy'.*

# XVII

# A letter from your old addiction

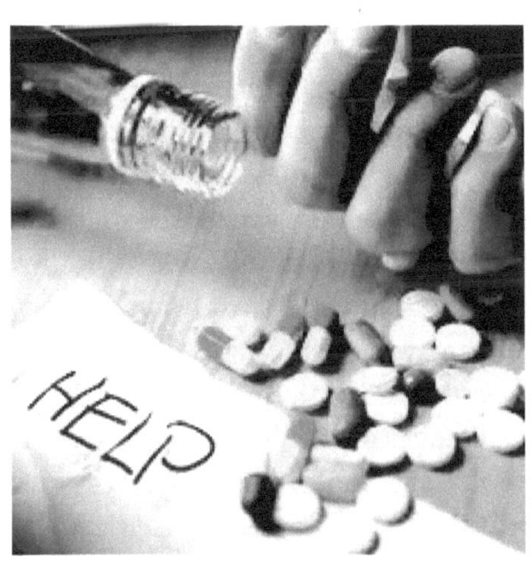

*I didn't win because I am sober, I won because I never quit trying*

Dear Addict,

It's been so long since I have seen you. Last time when I saw you, you were completely mesmerised by me. You were so in love with me. You were hugging me. I was with you in so many forms. Sometimes in an injection, sometimes in a bottle, sometimes in the form of tablets. But in any form or shape, you still loved me. You did not judge me by my Color, form, shape or how expensive or cheap I was. You loved me anyway.

Remember the days when you used to wake up with me. I was the first thing on your mind when you woke up and then you would hold me in your body. You were so in love with me. I colored you in my colors, mixed your emotions, thinking and life in my flavours. I made you feel on top of the world. I made you feel like a leader, like a damn ruler. You got such a high every time you were with me. Every time you kissed me, you went to a fantasy land. You couldn't live without me even for an hour. You were in my grip and you didn't want to break free. Ours was such an amazing bond. I lived because you kept me alive with you, in you.

That time when you lost your loved one, when you had life problems, when you faced issues with your money, when your partner left you – you always came back to me. I always comforted you. I was always there for you. Through all your tough times, you found your escape in me. When life threw challenges at you, you found solace in me. When you came to me, sad, lonely and depressed, I never let you down. I always gave you comfort, eased your pain and let you believe that it was alright. In exchange you gave me your health, your money, your happiness, your family and your life.

We had such an amazing relationship that I never thought that you could break free of me. We were so in love with each other. If we would have continued, it would have been till death do us apart. But now when I look at you, smiling without me, happy with your family and friends, a stable relationship with your special partner, I feel so lonely. You completely sidelined me. We didn't need anyone between us and we were happy but for you, I think that happiness was not enough. We were in our own world, my world.. but you wanted your world too. You wanted your life. The life I had created for us was so nice, full of fantasy, where we ruled everyday. But you wanted a 'real' life. You wanted a family, a stable relationship, money, goals and all these things got between us. You broke free from me, I wonder for how long. But now after so many years when I see you not returning to me, I feel what if you completely forgot me.

But no, then the other day you had me, you did drink me but just a sip or two. You found your boundaries and you kept them raise between you and me. I see now that you are not in my grip anymore. You have released yourself. You are no longer in my world, you have your own world. And I can see you shining. Those dark circles, that weak health, breathing problems all are gone. Those were the signs of our love but you left me and today you look like a completely new person. You look strong, beautiful and magnificent. You don't look like me, you look more like you. I don't know if you'll ever return back to me the same way that you were with me but if not, then I'll move on and find someone else.

I know there are many more who need me and not all are as strong as you. So Till then... am giving you your life back.

Goodbye,
Alcohol, drugs, prescription medicines.

# XVIII

## Are you in love with the idea of being in love OR Are you in love?

*I might not know what love is, but I surely know its not an illusion*

*What does love look like?*

Okay, before I begin with this topic, let me tell you that if you think love is all the pictures that are posted above, then think again. These pictures are the media imposed images of what love should look like. Laughing in the sunset, caressing the hair, smelling the roses, sitting on a park bench, clicking cute selfies are some things which we think people in love normally do. When these things don't happen in our relationships, we think our relationship is not perfect.

The image that love has on our mind is a preconceived notion of what we see in the movies. I am no exception when I say that movies have defined the way I look at love. We think that the person who we love or will fall in love with would be of a certain type, a certain stature, he/she will look good, have a decent earning, will speak well, will be respectful and oh my god, the list is never ending. But I want to ask all of us, so many expectations from one person. Really? That is so unfair to the person and also unfair to us.

Unfair to the person on who we keep our bags of expectations and unfair to us because we believe that we need another person to fulfill those expectations. If I talk about the list of things we like to see in an ideal parter- 1. looks: it's temporary and will fade away soon. 2. Earning: can't we do that for ourselves and infact even help uplift our family/partner. 3. Status: Again we can do that ourselves and create a name for ourselves.

So what exactly is that laundry list of 'ideal characteristics' in a partner for? I mean if all these expectations can be fulfilled by us, why the list? If you really go out looking for love with that list in your hand, you'll never find the one. And what good will a person with all these qualities be if he/she can't make you happy?

To think about it, the person that makes you happy is someone who truly loves you. Because except for a mother, the human mind is not trained for selfless loving. We always associate love to how it makes us feel. If we see 'our' happiness in someone, then we want to be with that person. No one would like to be with someone who doesn't make them or made them feel happy. In the end, it is all about how 'we' feel about someone where we define if we are in love or not. It is a complicated emotion where we associate love as an 'act of giving' to someone when in actuality it is 'we' who are making ourselves happy by being in love with the other person.

Selfless love is not humanly possible most times by people. So if you find someone who loves you for all your perfections and imperfections, your flaws and achievements, who will be there in all your good and bad times, who accepts you the way you are, hold that person to your dear life. He/she may not caress your hair, take you into the sunset, talk romantic with you, be good looking or earn well. But all that matters is that he/she loves you. Love begins within ourselves and only when we are filled with love can we give it to someone else. And the person I mentioned here my friend, may just be that one love you would be looking for ♥?

# XIX

# The dilemma of achieving happiness

*Happiness is a state of mind as we all know it to be*

What makes me happy?

In the Pursuit of happiness, are you loosing yourself?

Last week, I spoke to a friend. She had a lot of issues going on in her life, in her work, family and even in her relationship. Her work life was over-bearing its head in her personal life. She could not spend time with her family who felt ignored by her. She could not even completely concentrate on her work because she was facing relationship issues.

She faced some health issues and had to be hospitalized. It was during her hospitalization that she got the time to call me. She spoke about everything that was going on in her life.

Apparently, her boss did not appreciate her work. She was finding it difficult to fulfill her KPIs (Key Performance indicators). She was intimidated by her immediate new supervisor. She was also having some issues with her boyfriend who she felt was not giving her time and attention.

Her family had expectations from her and would ask her about future plans of marriage and settling down almost everyday. Somedays she used to lash out at them and some other days she understood their dilemma. She was completely disappointed in the way her life was going.

It was like climbing a wall that has become damp due to its continuous exposure to the rain water. She felt she was sliding heavily down in a dark tunnel with no other side to it. It took a toll on her health and she had heavy stress related blood pressure issues. When she spoke to me, she sounded so sad and disappointed that I never thought I could bring her back from there.

Sometimes when someone asks for your advice, they don't actually need it. What they need is for someone to be in their shoes, wear their lens, feel what they are feeling and understand how difficult it is to be them. I knew that advice wasn't something she was looking for, it was empathy. We both spoke about the disappointments that life gives us and why it should happen to any of us. She felt a little better and thanked me for 'not' giving her any advice and just listening.

To think about the heart of the matter, what disappoints us? A job? A failed relationship? A stressful family issue? All of these? Yes, they disappoint us because they are important to us. We associate them to making us happy. We all know that happiness is in our own hands but do we also know that as much as we want it to be in our hands, we can't let it stay there? Yes, happiness lies in our way of thinking but what if these thoughts lie on the bed of all of our life's priorities like love, family, money etc.?

Well, maybe we can put our happiness in the hands of our important people, but we should remember that at the end of the day, its always we who own it. This way, no matter who makes us happy, we always return it back to home i.e within ourselves ?

# XX

# The modern woman – Is she hiding somewhere?

*Being modern is to be able to express our thoughts without
supressing someone else's*

I don't need to introduce her to anyone – The 'modern
woman'. She is everywhere and she is everyone. She is
somebody's wife, sister, friend, mother, girlfriend,
daughter-in-law, sister-in-law, mother-in-law, mistress, boss,
employee, professional etc. She is everywhere – at home,
in office, in parks, gyms, cinema halls, malls and so many

other places. So how do you identify the modern woman?

Now when we look around, In office – we see her wearing smart attire with perfect makeup wearing heels trying to achieve the biased patriarchal world. At home we see her effortlessly multi-tasking trying to spread love around her. She is the one who makes the breakfast, handles the maids, gives attention to her kids, tries to please her husband all the time also trying to get glimpses of some new recipes on a social app.

She keeps a track of what is there in the house and what is to be bought all the time while also making that big pitch presentation. She is the one who manages it all and has the highest competency known to mankind.

But in all these things she does, in all the role she plays, she forgets to play the role of a woman. The woman that she is to herself. So many times does a woman sacrifices her own wishes that at times she even forgets she has many wishes. Wishing and fulfilling her wishes becomes a luxury to her so much that she doesn't even try to go that way. Also, when someone tries to fulfil them, she feels so grateful to that person. A small gesture to make her happy by someone is a big deal for her when she doesn't realise that she is doing multiple such sweet and small gestures towards everybody around her.

Women are very unfair to themselves. They try to do everything but ignore themselves. There are many times when a woman wants to come home from office and just sit on the sofa watching tv but she isn't able to do so. Many times she just wants to go out with her friends and stay the night. There are so many times she wants to go on a solo trip somewhere. But these are the bigger things. Lets talk about the small things. She is not even able to get the small things like getting ready breakfast in bed, coming home to a cooked dinner, going out for drinks.

The society forgets that she is a woman first then is all the roles that she plays. Women are even made to forget their desires, fantasies and the fact that they are allowed to play out their fantasies. When I see this 'modern woman' around me, I can only wonder how lost she is? Why can't the modern woman do as she likes? I mean as she really likes? Because of the preconceived notions that other 'modern women' like herself make about their roles. Because of the fact that her mothers and their mothers advised her to do 'what is best for her'.

So you see, if we really want a change in this so called 'being modern' concept, it starts from the older generation of women. If we keep sustaining the preconceived notions of the society on how our life should be and how we should live it or if we go by their definition of 'what a successful woman looks like' we would imply all these expectations to our future generations.

It is time to break the chain and define the reality of the 'modern woman'. What is her reality? Who is the 'modern woman'?

I'd say she is whoever the hell she wants to be!

# XXI
# Traits of a strong woman

# So stronger

*It is me who defines my strength!*

If you know any strong women or they have been amongst your family and/or friends or if you are a strong woman, you will be able to relate to most of the points mentioned in this post. I couldn't wait for woman's day to write this because being a woman shouldn't just be celebrated in one day.

Womanhood is a privilege which most of us don't realize. I have seen women trying to exploit it, some who have tried to hate it, some have even tried to change it and some have tried to go into a self-pity box with it (I hate this category). However, women are special, Period

What most women don't realize is, that how strong we are. That is precisely the reason why we were chosen to bring a new life. We have strength, endurance, empathy, confidence and we carry it all underneath our pretty eyelashes and cute faces (Can it get any better than that ?). All said, what are those things that make us strong? What are the top traits of a strong woman? I checked with a few strong women on the secret behind 'how they do it' and thought to put together this list:

1. Strong women cry:

Yes, as surprising as it sounds, strong women do cry. The only difference is that they don't cry in front of anyone. When something bad happens, they cry their heart out to themselves, try to console themselves and then move on. Crying helps them to move on.

2. They face their issues:

Strong women know that life will throw problems at you and you gotta deal with it. They don't panic at the face of problems and know that panic or stress doesn't solve issues but rather ignite them further.

3. They stand for themselves:

Strong women realize their worth and don't take any disrespectful treatement. If anyone does that, they react once and later will make sure to delete that person forever. Nobody disrespects them, that is for certain.

4. They are self-made:

Strong women create their own path. They face all challenges and emerge as a new person. They keep their achievements safely as remembrance to their positive points and apply them as and when they get a chance.

5. They know their weaknesses:

Strong women know that they don't know-it-all. They are aware that they are not perfect and there is still room for improvement. Hence, they work towards improving and progressing.

6. They are original:

Unlike most people these days, strong women are original. Original in thought, action and their promises. Yes, that is true. They make promises which they know they can fulfill and hence don't overdo it. In this, their promises are customized.

7. They are kind:

Strong women are empathetic. Empathy is one of the biggest trait of a protector and strong women are very good protectors. Therefore, it is evident that they are also empathetic. However, they know the difference between a real problem and a petty issue. Hence, don't expect their empathy on something which they don't feel is a problem to start with.

8. They empower:

Being independent is so often misinterpreted. Being independent not only means depending on yourself but also means not to create any dependency. Strong women don't just know this but also apply it, thus empowering whatever or whomever they be with.

9. They are confident:

Strong women are confident even with all their flaws. They know they may not be the most intelligent or beautiful or charming one in the room but they accept themselves with their flaws confidently.

10. They set an example:

Every strong woman sets an example to her fellow gender members and inspires them to be like her. There is no denying that she is awesome and an original wanted to be copied by so many ?

Are you a strong woman or do you know any? If yes, then know that you are special and the world needs more women like you. More power to you!

• 89 •

# XXII

# Beauty and the brains

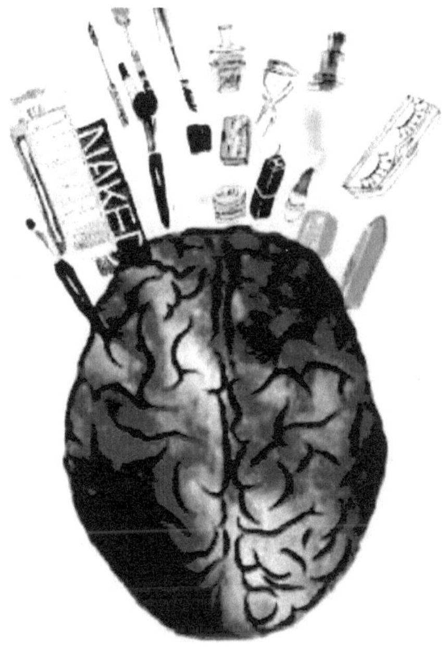

*Beauty wins the battle but brain is the legendary hero winning the war*

This blog is fairly different then 'Beauty and the Beast' as is obvious from the title. Unlike the fairy tale, in the real world as we all know (or assume), beauty normally doesn't fall in love with brains. Beauty is attracted to beauty unless she realizes the amazing perception of the brain.

I am surrounded with tons of ladies who are constantly trying to change their appearance. To be honest, I also keep trying the new and not-so-true beauty products in an attempt to maybe change the way my hair looks, the way my skin feels, the way I smell and the way I dress-up

So, are we all prone to get fooled by the marketing gimmicks of companies? I'd say, yes to that. And are we all prone to get fooled by external apperances? I'd again say yes to that. Does that mean that we all value beauty over brains? I'd say no. While beauty is a pleasure to the eyes, brains are truly fascinating. Beauty doesn't know how under-valued she would be if brains enter the playing field. While beauty can get you from A to B, brains can break any limitations so much that you realize that the so-called B is just a start of your journey to success. In the world of brains, there is no A or B. There is just a steep mountain of exploration where your curiosity will take you to higher and higher altitudes. And the higher you go, the more the atmospheric pressure around your beauty drops. Then at a certain level, the beauty in you stops breathing.

You get a new confidence. Something which beauty couldn't have given you. So much is the power of brain that as opposed to beauty, the more you undress or decode a certain topic, the higher your respect level increases. Brains also have another advantage – They never age. Beauty is temporary and may fade away with time but brain is what people will fall in love with again and again.

Beauty comes with a price but brains will increase your value. The ROI on brain is very high as compared to the investment of never stopping to learn. However, there is one advantage of beauty over brains – while beauty doesn't need to be shown off as it is pretty obvious if a person is *externally* beautiful or not, brain on the other hand, if not applied practically will never come in the limelight. Brain is that silent child which needs introduction to every party it goes to, but once it plays its magic, be rest assured that it has left a mark.

Beauty is comparable. There will always be another girl/ guy more beautiful/charming than you. However brain is unique. You either have it or not. And trust me, when you are perceived as the woman who has brains, your beauty takes a back seat where you happily wanna keep it there. Brain automatically even increases your beauty and people who already perceive you as intelligent get attracted to your beauty (with whatever compromised state it is in) as well. You might not be the most beautiful girl in the room but you surely become unique to people because you then become the rare but perfect package of 'Beauty and the Brains'.

So ladies, when you are slathering on those creams and those parlor visits and spending expensive bucks on fairness treatments, also invest in some curious endeavors where you constantly keep learning

Give Brains a chance ?

# XXIII

# What Lies Beneath The LIES

*Lie is an honest cover to prevent the truth from escalating things*

Well, lets be honest for a while. We all lie. Those who say that they dont lie, are lying. Maybe 90% of the time they dont lie, but 10% lies are spoken by everyone. Lies dont always mean bad though. Most people lie to stop hurting other people. Some of us lie because people cant hear the truth. Some of us lie because it gets our work done. We lie when its convenient for us. We lie when we can't speak the truth. We lie when we can't let truth ruin our relationships. We lie on small things, we lie on big deals.

Corporates are full of lies. They lie while hiring and they lie when firing. They lie during promotions and they lie during demotions. Advertisements are lies wrapped in a fancy cover served to us with a price tag. People lie through their words and also through their actions. So whoever said 'Actions speak louder than words', strictly confined it to the truth, because lies dominate both forms.

The one thing common in humans is that most of the times, we fall for the lies. We accept lies as truth and then act surprised when we hear the truth. We feel fooled when lied to, but we go out there in the world and lie ourselves. Lies is more a part of our lives then truth can be and I think that is why truth is so much more valued. Kids dont lie. Lies are not taught in school. Lies are too complicated for kids to handle and hence they can't lie. However, since they are kids, their truth, no matter however bitter, is always forgotten and forgiven.

So, why is the world full of lies. Probably because lies is what relaxes us? Soothes us? Hides the bitter truth? Ofcourse yes! Thats why corporates use it for their benefits and marketers almost exploit it. Lies spoken confidently sound so much like the truth. These kinda lies create a chain of lies where the carrier is the person who hears the lie and believes it to be true. He or she then passes it further unknowingly thinking that it is the truth.

Even when we say we love to hear the truth, I'd be lying if I said I dont like lies. For instance, if a friend lies to me about me losing my weight and looking amazing, I would like it. If she suddenly thinks about me when she needs a favor, I'd gloat in her 'lied' remembrance of me.

The truth is that lies make most of our lives convenient. Lies are very under-rated because they relax us. They make us stress-free. They free us from bondages. But beware, lies are only so good as long they dont completely erode the truth. Truth is much stronger than lies. Lies may not be forgiven but truth can never be forgotten. Truth overpowers lies in the long run. Truth removes the blinds of temporary happiness created by lies and brings sunshine into the room.

So why lie? I believe lies should only be used as a solution once in a while to make life a little easier. The destination should always be the truth. Lies should only be used when we want to ease things out a little to pave the way for the truth. Lies can be a part of life but definitely not a way of life. Lies should be harmless. How do we ensure that? Simply by understanding the intentions behind the lies. We need to know that something 'good' lies beneath the lies we speak ?

# About The Author

VAIKHARI CHAVAN-NAIK
VAIKHARI IS AN IT PROFESSIONAL WORKING WITH AN MNC FIRM. SHE IS ALSO AN AUTOMATION SPECIALIST AND A BUSINESS PROCESS RISK CONSULTANT. SHE WAS ALWAYS CURIOUS ABOUT HER WRITING SKILLS AND WANTED TO EXPLORE THE WRITER UNDERNEATH HER TECHNICAL SKILLS. THIS IS HER ATTEMPT TOWARDS LISTENING TO THE INNER WRITER WITHIN AND GIVING THAT WRITER A CHANCE